Refugee to Restaurateur:

The Amazing Survival Story of Thao Te

By

Thao Te

As narrated to Dr Darryl Cross

Cover design by Nu-Image Design

Published by Crossways Publishing:
    PO Box 2000, North Adelaide SA
    Australia 5006

ISBN: 0-9806101-9-2

ISBN-13: 978-0-9806101-9-2

Disclaimer

The author denies any liability for incidental or consequential damages resulting from the use of the information in this book. This book is designed simply to tell a personal story relating to one's own journey. It does not make decisions for the individual or in any way is meant to be prescriptive for how others might live their lives. It is simply a personal narrative. No responsibility is accepted for any liabilities resulting from the actions of any parties involved.

It is also noted that this publication is designed to provide accurate and authoritative information with regard to the subject matter covered. It is sold and offered with the understanding that the author is not engaged in rendering legal, accounting or financial advice of any kind. If legal advice, advice relating to mental health issues or any other professional assistance is required, the services of a competent professional in the appropriate area should be sought.

As far as is possible, the names of the various cities, towns, places and people are accurate. No responsibility is taken for any inaccuracies in this regard.

Acknowledgments

An autobiography of this nature does just not happen without the valuable services and skills of various individuals.

Many thanks to Beth Nixon for her hours of work initially transcribing the many interviews that I had with Te over a year or more and her diligent work in locating place names, towns and localities. Thanks to Karina Ellis in using her creative talents in coming up with a briefer title than the one that I originally had in mind. Thanks to Gwen Hoffnagle for all her diligent work in proof-reading and editing. Her continued attention to detail and her efficiency in meeting deadlines was refreshing.

I am grateful for the assistance afforded by Richard Banham in his ability to use software and particularly in relation to formatting issues which can be the bane of almost everyone's life at times. I am thankful too that he is an Apple fan.

I am indebted too to my wife Billie who continued to support this whole endeavour and who understood that there were times when I was necessarily laptop-bound for extended periods over a couple of years.

Finally, thank you to the man himself, Te, who not only keenly gave of his time and energy to this project, but who was called upon to revisit memories from his past, painful memories that were difficult to recount, and at times so difficult that he did not wish to go there.

Darryl

ii

Foreword

You've no doubt heard about *"the killing fields."* You may have seen the film. It was horrible enough on the big screen – the inhumanity of man to man, of person to person.

But most of us live lives of luxury, at least comparative luxury. And in our busy 21st century lives, we are far removed from both the past and the present atrocities that occur on our planet. Every once in a while though, there is a glimpse into those other lives of desperation and tragedy, despair and agony. Every now and again, if we allow ourselves, we come face-to-face with not only what has occurred, but what is occurring every day of our lives but is just not in our vicinity, locality or neighbourhood. Thank God.

For a year or more, my wife Billie and I ate regularly in Te's Thai restaurant just a few doors down from our office. It wasn't that it was just convenient; the food was really good and the staff were always pleasant and agreeable.

As it happened, we got to know Te, the owner, and later his wonderful wife Sanom. Actually, his name is Thao Te, but as is the tradition in his homeland of Cambodia, he goes by his last name. Everyone here in Oz thinks it's his first name.

One night after a very enjoyable meal, Te pulled up a chair for a chat. He does that often with some of his regular customers. I'm not sure how we got onto it, but a small part of his story began to emerge. He became tearful and we began to see the enormity of the tragedy and the agony that he had endured. It affected both of us profoundly.

On other occasions when we visited the restaurant, more of this story unfolded. At some point, it just seemed obvious that

Te needed to tell his story more publicly. It was an inspiring story of survival; the story of how his grandmother had prepared the way for his survival; the story of the remarkable ability of this man to survive the killing fields, of being reunited with most of his family against all odds and now to be serving his customers in his amicable, friendly yet humble manner. A gracious man indeed. An awesome man indeed.

How was it that Te survived the atrocities in his homeland? How did he manage to find other members of his family? How did he find his way out of a refugee camp to be selected to come to Australia? How did he come to be a highly respected restaurateur? Was it just luck or was it God's hand or something else? Te believes that he has been spiritually guided...there seems to be little other explanation.

But Te is not one for writing or putting down his experiences on paper. He is a restaurateur and a darn good one at that. So I asked him if he would like to record some of his tales in order to tell his whole story. He was keen on the idea and so the story unravelled.

It was a real privilege to hear his story, and humbling. It is a constant reminder of how blessed we are living in a Westernised society and in a democracy in a privileged country like Australia.

The shame on us that we take it all for granted. The shame on us that we whinge and moan about all sorts of inconsequential and somewhat petty things to do with the trivialities of life. The shame on us that we don't make the most of what we have in life, and instead tend to focus more on the negatives.

When we hear and read Te's story, it helps us to get life in perspective again. It helps us understand that there is a bigger force than us guiding our lives and this planet.

This book is dedicated to an inspiring champion of a man called Thao Te. A champion indeed.

Dr Darryl Cross

Contents

Acknowledgements   (i)
Foreword   (iii)
Preface   (ix)
Contents   (vii)

Chapter 1:   Life Before the Killing Fields   1

Chapter 2:   The War Comes to Cambodia   9

Chapter 3:   First Capture by the Khmer Rouge
              – The 100 days   11

Chapter 4:   Second Capture
              – Survival in the Killing Fields   17

Chapter 5:   Death All Around – 1975-77   21

Chapter 6:   Survival – 1977-79   29

Chapter 7:   Vietnamese Army Liberates   33

Chapter 8:   Our First Thailand Refugee Camp
              – Finding Part of My Family   39

Chapter 9:   Our Second Thailand Refugee Camp
              – Finding My Natural Sisters   51

Chapter 10:   Touchdown in Australia   61

Chapter 11:   The Start of the Restaurants   69

Chapter 12:   Finding My Father   87

Chapter 13:   My Family in Australia   91

Preface

For generations Cambodia endured civil battles. In 1970, General Lon Nol deposed Prince Norodom Sihanouk, who had kept Cambodia out of the war between North and South Vietnam by granting concessions to appease both sides. At the time, America was fighting in Vietnam.

With the Prince gone, Cambodia declared war on North Vietnam and the Americans were ordered into Cambodia by President Nixon to support the Cambodians against Hanoi, though President Nixon, not trusting General Lon Nol, forgot to mention this to him until the deployment and invasion were completed.[1] The Soviets backed Hanoi, and Cambodia became a pawn of the major powers that fought the Cold War using Cambodia as a battleground.

Meanwhile, China backed the Khmer Rouge, the Cambodian communist movement. With this Chinese backing and tutelage, the Khmer Rouge grew in status and recruitment power from a motley collection of ineffectual guerrilla bands in 1965 of, at most, 3,000 to 5,000 men into a murderous force of 70,000 to 100,000 men.

---

[1] Samuel Lipsman, Edward Doyle, et al. *"Fighting for Time."* Boston: Boston Publishing Company, 1983, p. 127.

This three-way battle between China, the Soviet Union and the United States of America allowed the Khmer Rouge to grow to become a larger and better financed force. The power the Khmer Rouge were then able to wield resulted in a more ruthless force than would have been the case, as the commentators argue, if the Americans had not entered the battle.

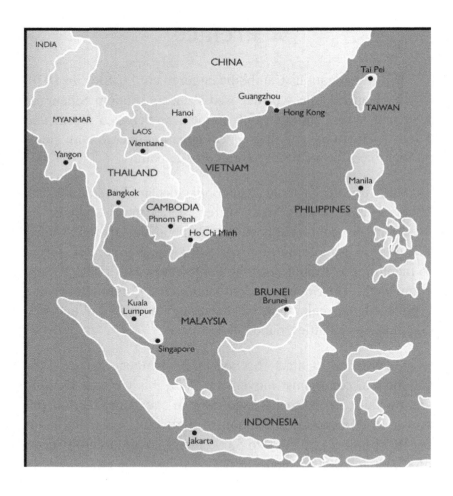

In April of 1975, the crowds cheered as the Khmer Rouge marched into Phnom Penh in Cambodia.[2] At the helm was their leader, Pol Pot. Within days, Pol Pot's regime plundered and killed and forcibly evacuated cities to create a brutal agrarian society in which intellectuals, professionals, government officials, ethnic Chinese and many others were murdered in what became known as the killing fields. Estimates of the death toll vary from 1.7 million to as high as three million (about 20% of the population).

The devastation that Pol Pot wreaked on his country is hard to comprehend, even three decades later. His goal, as he put it, was to return Cambodia to "year zero" and transform it into an agrarian utopia. To that end, he purged his nation of educated city dwellers, monks and minorities, while imposing a draconian resettlement program that uprooted almost everyone else. These measures led to the deaths of at least a quarter of the country's population.

Then, on Christmas Day in 1978, Vietnam invaded and the Khmer Rouge were gone within a fortnight.[3] A puppet government was installed in which one Hun Sen was the foreign minister. When Vietnamese forces pulled out ten years later, they left behind several Cambodian factions battling for control. Then, in 1991, these factional groups' leaders signed a United Nations sponsored peace accord, giving Cambodia the extraordinary opportunity to start over. The country's new constitution awarded Cambodians human rights, personal freedoms and other protections of a modern democratic state. And in 1993, the UN staged a national election to select a democratic government. After the horrors of the Khmer Rouge,

---

[2] *"The Advertiser,"* Friday, 1st January, 2010, Page 19

[3] http://www.cambodiangenocide.org/genocide.htm. Retrieved 3rd February, 2011

Cambodia would remake itself at last, and its people would have a chance to thrive.

However, in the 18 years since that election, the government has squandered that opportunity. Hun Sen came in second in the 1993 election, but muscled his way into the government nevertheless. Interestingly, Hun Sen was originally a leader in the Khmer Rouge regime. Four years later, he staged a coup. Since then, his government has been looting Cambodia's natural resources, jailing political opponents, kicking thousands of the weakest out of their homes, and fostering an expansive system of corruption, all the while ignoring challenges and complaints from organisations and governments around the world.

About 80% of Cambodia's 14 million people live in rural villages in very deprived conditions. The government acknowledges that only 16% of the population has toilets, leaving the rest – some 12 million men, women and children – to defecate outside, over the aquifers from which they draw water for drinking, cooking and bathing.[4]

Many people in Phnom Penh and other cities distain Hun Sen and the members of his political party for living far beyond their official means. Although a minister's salary is about US$300 a month, Hun Sen is building himself a four-storey mansion the size of a suburban office building with a heliport on the roof. While it is under construction, Hun Sen is staying at his country estate which has a private golf course. But Cambodians in the countryside seldom see any evidence of this ill-gotten bounty. The government controls all the television stations; although newspapers are relatively independent, they do not circulate outside the cities; and,

---

[4] Prof Joel Brinkley, The Review, "*The Australian Financial Review*," Friday, 3rd April, 2009, Page 1-2, 10.

according to the government, only about 3% of the population has access to the Internet.

The US Embassy in Cambodia has made anti-corruption a priority in its relationship with the Hun Sen government. It funded two comprehensive studies that were published in 2004 and 2005. They showed in stunning detail that Cambodian government officials steal between US$300 million and US$500 million a year. (Most years, the state's annual budget is about US$1 billion.)

International donors, in other words, are in effect bankrolling the Cambodian state, despite economic growth rates that until recently exceeded 10%. Former US Ambassador Mussomeli says these figures were less impressive than they seemed because Cambodia's recent growth started from "a very low base." At the same time, Cambodia's economy relies on three principal sources of income: textiles, tourism and agriculture. Its reliance on textiles is so extreme, in fact, that Cambodia has become beholden to US retailers. As Mussomeli put it, "Levi Strauss or The Gap could destroy this country on a whim.[5]"

In 2005 however, oil and natural gas deposits were found beneath Cambodia's territorial waters, and once commercial extraction begins in 2011, the oil revenues could profoundly affect Cambodia's economy.[6]

Regardless, Cambodia has floundered because of a government steeped in corruption, and with world attention now focused on other sites such as Iraq and Afghanistan, what

---

[5] Prof Joel Brinkley, The Review, "*The Australian Financial Review,*" Friday, 3rd April, 2009, Page 10.

[6] Ed Madra, Cambodia hopes to start oil production in 2009. Reuters. http://www.reuters.com/article/2007/01/19/oil-cambodia-idUSBKK30404620070119 Retrieved 2nd April, 2011

incentive is there for bringing transparency to government spending in Cambodia?

Chapter 1
Life Before the Killing Fields

Thao Te was born on the first of October, 1959, in Phnom Penh, the capital of Cambodia. "Te" is actually his last name, but when he first came to Australia and people asked him his name, he answered with his last name as was the custom in Cambodia. Now, in Australia, he is known as "Te," and he is happy to be known in this way. He was the third child to two elder sisters, Lang and Suree. His brother Chheng was born much later. It is also important to mention that his dad had two wives. Te also had three half-sisters and two half-brothers from his half-mother, whose name was Tang Huy Chuy.

He was told that on his first birthday his family held the biggest party they had ever had because his father had the best year ever in business during 1959 and1960.

One of his earliest memories is from when he was about six years old in 1965 and living with his father, mother, half-mother and the seven other children in Phnom Penh. He was in school at that time where he was taught English because it was

1

near the Thai border. If he had attended school near the Vietnamese border, he would have been taught French. He doesn't have many memories of Phnom Penh and growing up there though – he was still very young.

"My father knew that Cambodia was probably pretty much unstable. The Khmer Rouge Movement was around the country at the time and so my father took all of us children from Phnom Penh to a border town in Northwest Cambodia called Poipet." Poipet was right across the border from Thailand. Some maps show the spelling as Paoy Paet (see the map on the next page).

"I was about seven years of age then. There were nine children altogether by that time – four with my natural mum and five from my step-mum. My father thought it would be safer for us to be in a border town where we could maybe escape to Thailand if necessary.

We did business very well from the day that we arrived. Dad knew somebody there, so, of course, the business went well. We had a store in Poipet which was involved in selling household goods, furniture, food, spices, flowers, sugar, craft and home décor – pretty much everything really. In a sense, we acted like a middle-man, on-selling goods. We would source goods from China, Vietnam and Cambodia and sell the products in Thailand."

They did most of their trade between the Thai and Cambodia markets. They travelled between Poipet and the area known as Aranyaprathet in Thailand, which runs along the Thai border and is just across from Poipet.

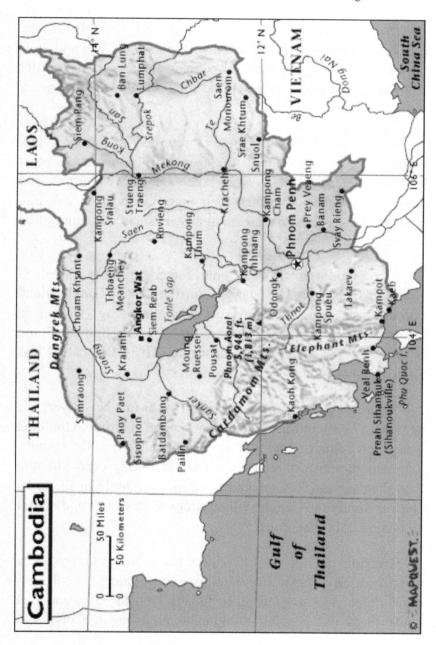

They would buy goods in Thailand to sell to the Cambodians, and on the weekends it was almost like a kind of duty-free business. Busloads of people came across the border from Thailand, not to mention the train which arrived twice a week.

Te's father and natural mother returned to Phnom Penh, which is about 700 kilometres from the border and Poipet (about the same distance from Adelaide to Melbourne), and stayed there where they had their main business. It was like having a head office in the capital city. His dad and mum often visited them in Poipet.

Te's grandmother, Tang, his father's mother, lived in Kokolot, which was well back from the Cambodian-Thailand border. It is a small town west of Battambang (written as Batdambang on the adjacent map) on National Highway 5 and is too small to be shown on most maps. It is also called Kas Kralo or Koas Krala.

"Grandpa died when I was about five or maybe six years of age. He was about ninety-four years old at the time. Grandma was much younger than him as was the custom in the country that men married women about fifteen or twenty years younger than themselves. So Grandma lived in the middle of the town and her family took up the whole street with aunties and uncles all up and down the street.

Grandma did not like us children being brought up in a city and organised for us to live with her in the country. She did not think Poipet was a good place for children to be educated. I know that's old peoples' thinking about being too civilised. What I mean is that she thought that children grew up too fast in the city. She really wanted me to stay close and be educated in a country town. I grew up with her until I was about eleven or twelve years old when I then moved back to the border town of Poipet. I think that I was probably one of her favourite grandsons and I feel that's why she wanted me to stay close to her.

It was wonderful being so close to Grandma because she would tell me bedtime stories and she played and talked to me like a mother. So, I really grew up in Kokolot. I went to school in Kokolot where we had thirty children in the class all aged from eight to twelve years and I finished my primary schooling there.

I think I was probably a slow learner and if I couldn't understand something, the teacher would hit me mostly across the back with a bamboo stick. I'd come home with blood all over my shirt from the teacher beatings. Grandma would get so angry saying, 'What sort of a teacher is he?' And he was a Buddhist monk, too! The children were all afraid of him.

Grandma got so mad at one stage that she went down to the school to tell him off. The teacher couldn't say anything because Grandma was a respected woman in the community."

Later in Te's schooling however, he became very good at mathematics. He astounded the teacher with the speed at which he could do maths. No one in the class could beat him.

This picture is taken outside Grandmother's house and is Te's half-mother's side of the family. Grandmother sits proudly in the front row second from the left. Back row on the far right is Te's half-mother (Tang Huy Chuy) and next to her with the sunglasses is Te's father. Standing in front of Te's father is Te's eldest half-sister Bouy and in front of her is his half-brother Hung Chang who was later killed by the Khmer Rouge. At this stage, Te was not yet born when the photo was taken.

"Grandma was an amazing lady. She was always about business. She started from scratch and built up a rice farm, rice factory, chicken farm and pig farm. We had thousands of pigs. Grandmother was tough but loving. She would tell me, 'Always keep busy and don't be lazy.' She was a person who always tried to help everyone go in the right direction for them. Grandma and my half-brother, Hung Chang, educated me in life and taught me many things. In a way though, I lost my childhood in that I never had any playtime – it was always about work.

My half-brother taught me a lot on the farms. We never wasted anything. I would feed leftovers from the rice factory to the chickens and the pigs. I would collect fresh eggs early each morning, both chicken and duck eggs, and take them to market to sell. Fresh eggs would sell very quickly and they'd all be gone in thirty to forty minutes. Then I'd go to school. After school, I'd work in the garden because we had a herb garden as well. I was always busy. At night I'd also have to do some homework.

I owe my life to that lady who taught all of us children about life, and the communists, and what to expect and watch out for. And she taught us how to work. She is my hero and her photo stands proudly over the counter area in my restaurant today. Grandma is still watching over me."

Grandma Tang's photo in the restaurant.

When Te was about eleven years old, in 1970, the Khmer Rouge started to invade small country towns around Phnom Penh. After living in Kokolot with his grandmother, he spent his initial teenage years – until 1975 – back in Poipet.

Chapter 2
The War Comes to Cambodia

Te and his family knew that there were trouble spots around the country with the Khmer Rouge. It was one of the reasons his father had the foresight to move his family closer to the Thai border to Poipet. But how did Te see the conflict around him? What was his explanation for what was occurring in his country?

"Fighting in Cambodia started in the 1960s, at the same time as the Vietnam War. The Khmer Rouge waged attacks against South Vietnam. North Vietnam was already fighting South Vietnam, so North Vietnam and the Khmer Rouge fought South Vietnam together. The Khmer Rouge were supported by China, and Cambodia and South Vietnam supported each other. Though fighting was going on all around Cambodia, in the beginning it didn't impact life near the Thai border or near us because it was so far away from Vietnam.

The war started on the North Vietnamese border, but then came down into Phnom Penh and to Angkor Wat[7], the famous temple complex in Cambodia. In March of 1975, the Americans pulled out of Cambodia and Vietnam, allowing North Vietnam to conquer South Vietnam. Then in April, the Khmer Rouge invaded Cambodia.

Vietnam didn't want to ally with China anymore, but with Russia instead. Vietnam didn't want to pay the debt it owed to China for helping them during the war with the Americans, so they went to war knowing the Russians would back them up.

After that struggle ended in 1978, Vietnam invaded Cambodia in 1979 because the Khmer Rouge had remained allies with China and had aided China against Vietnam, killing thousands of Vietnamese people near the border."

It took the Vietnamese soldiers three months to wipe out the Khmer Rouge, although most of it was done within two weeks.

---

[7] Angkor Wat lies 5.5 km north of the modern town of Siem Reap, and was built for King Suryavarman II in the early 12th Century as his state temple and capital city. It is in an area of Cambodia where there is an important group of ancient structures. It is the southernmost of Angkor's main sites.

Chapter 3
First Capture by the Khmer Rouge – The 100 Days

In 1973, Te had gone back to Kokolot with his younger brother Chheng to visit his grandmother on her birthday. She was quite old but still very clever and entrepreneurial. She and Te's cousin were managing the rice factory. There were two of Te's other families there – his mother's cousin's family and his father's sister's family. However, the Khmer Rouge invaded the town while he and Chheng were visiting.

The Khmer Rouge were not completely successful in taking over Kokolot because government forces pushed them back. However they did capture all the people that lived in the town. They forcibly removed Te and his family from their homes and did not allow them to take anything with them.

"They said, 'Just follow the troops to the mountain,' but we had no idea where we were going. The mountain and jungle area was where the Khmer Rouge lived and had their fortresses and hideouts, because they were raging guerrilla warfare

11

against the government. So we had no idea where we would end up.

As we were marching to the mountain area, we were separated into two groups. In my group there was my brother and myself, my auntie and my auntie's friend who lived close to us. In the other group were Grandma, my half-brother, my cousin and my niece. There were also three other workers who were like housekeepers. They looked after Grandma, which is why they all walked together in one group. Our group walked farther on and got separated from Grandma's group because Grandma was quite ill. I didn't know how bad she really was but she was very old at that time, around ninety-seven or ninety-eight. She could still walk okay though, but slowly.

Halfway to the jungle and the mountains, still with no idea where we were going, it began getting dark. Quite suddenly, one of the very young Khmer Rouge soldiers ran straight up to my auntie and said, 'Are you Miss Tang's family?' My auntie said, 'Yes, what's the problem?'

He said to my auntie, 'Look if you are Miss Tang's family, you had better walk faster. No matter what, walk faster.' My auntie asked, 'Why? Why do we have to walk faster?'

He said, 'I can't tell you any more, but you need to walk as fast as possible and don't stop!' My auntie kept asking him, 'Why? What is the matter? What is going on?' But he said, 'I can't answer any more questions,' and he ran off into the jungle.

I didn't know what was going on. Much later on I realised that he was really trying to warn us and save my family because he already knew the Khmer Rouge had captured my

Grandma and my half-brother and my cousin – the group that was somewhere behind us – and that the Khmer Rouge had already slaughtered and shot them. Did this soldier know my family somehow in that he was trying to warn us? We didn't know at all what was happening to us or who was who.

The next morning, we were just wandering around in this jungle mountain area when we met a family that knew my auntie. The man in this family also knew my Grandma very well. He was nice to us and it was he who really saved my family at this time when we got captured by the Khmer Rouge. Apparently, Grandma had helped him a lot when he was farming. She had loaned him some land, a cow, and all sorts of things so that he could farm. He said my Grandma had helped him a great deal and he saw this as the perfect time for him to repay those debts. He helped my family, and provided whatever he could during this difficult time.

During those first one hundred days of being captured by the Khmer Rouge, we really had no idea what was going to be. As refugees, we never thought about how we were going to get out at all. We just lived life day by day, wandering through whatever cornfield or potato field we could, trying to get something to eat, because under the Khmer Rouge regime, you didn't have your land anymore to grow rice or anything because you were living in a guerrilla war zone. We all lived in the jungle with the Khmer Rouge.

It was one hundred days after we were first captured by the Khmer Rouge that the government troops, along with some American soldiers, came up the mountain to where the hot spots of the Khmer Rouge were known to be. There was a lot of fighting and in the end the government and American troops won that area back.

We were in that territory that was re-captured, and we were set free again! Therefore we were able to then get back to our town, Kokolot, which is where our factory and house were. But our house had been burnt down, the factory was burnt down – everything was gone.

It was then that we found out that Grandma had been killed, along with my half-brother Hung Chang, my cousin, my niece and the rest of the workers.

It was then, too, that we realised and remembered the young Khmer Rouge fighter who had tried to warn us. He had come out of the jungle and told us to walk faster and not stop because he knew that if we did not move fast enough that we would be killed and executed just like Grandma was.

I found out about this exactly three months and ten days after the young Khmer Rouge soldier warned us. I asked people where they actually killed my Grandma and my family, the actual spot, but sadly, no one knew.

I still remember when I first heard the news that the Khmer Rouge had killed Grandma. I cannot describe the emotion that I felt. It was heartbreaking. It was like I had just lost my mother.

A close-up of Grandma Tang.

With everything in Grandma's town gone and with Grandma now dead, us children went back to our parents' business in Poipet near the border of Thailand and Cambodia. This was, as I've said, where my parents had a wholesale business which was a bit like a Bunnings store in Australia."

From 1973 until 1975, from the time Te was fourteen to when he was sixteen, he attended school and worked in the store. He would open the shop early at around 6.00 to 6.30am and then go to school from 8.30 to 3.00pm. After school, he would work in the shop again. The border crossing would shut around 6.00 to 6.30pm, so that meant most of the shopping would cease. At night the family would spend time packaging and preparing products and re-packing bulk products for sale.

He had worked in the shop since he had been eleven years old. Dealing with all the different kinds of nationalities that came into the shop meant that he learnt to speak Chinese and Thai and was exposed to other languages as well. He didn't know it then, but that was going to be a major benefit in his survival.

Chapter 4
Second Capture –
Survival in the Killing Fields

In March of 1975, Te's father and mother went back to Phnom Penh and Te, his half-mother and the eight other children stayed in Poipet. In April, war started again. This time the Khmer Rouge took over the country. They came to Te's home and gave the families three days to leave their houses and businesses. They told them that the Americans were going to bomb the town. "You stay and you die," they said at the time, and Te's family believed them.

They told them to leave as soon as possible and not take anything with them except a few items of clothing – that they would only need to stay away for a couple of days. They went forty or fifty kilometres to a place called Donorang (Te is not sure of the spelling) and were able to find refuge at a farmhouse. After a week they realised they had been lied to and that they would never get their homes back – and they had left everything behind. There were thousands of people who

17

had left their homes. They were all scared and didn't know what was true or what to do. After two weeks, Te's family was told to move on to another town.

"When we arrived, there were thousands of people there who had been starving for months. We thought, 'Gee, are we going to be starved here, too?' When we arrived at this town, we thought, 'This is not good.' But they said, 'You'll have to go and do what the other people do,' which is basically become slave labour. We just had to do what they told us to do, so for everyone it was the farm work. We worked the rice paddies and anything we could do like picking and chopping. It's all manual labour. There was hardly any food around so my mother said to me, 'What are we going to do, because if we carry on like this we are all going to die.' It was very, very hard for us to survive.

It was about three months after the April invasion that the Khmer Rouge started to separate us out and begin the 'cleansing.' One of the main ways of cleansing was to starve people to death because then the soldiers did not need to waste bullets and would simply overwork them until they got sick and died.

I was fifteen years of age. My younger brother Chheng was about ten years. Mum said to me that I was probably one of the smarter boys in the family at the time. She said to me that I had to be a survivor because in Cambodia we believe a boy must take on the family name to the next generation and so he must survive. This was important because the Chinese believed that if the boy lived on, the family would live on as well. [Te's family was of Chinese heritage.] It was important that I carry on the family bloodline. Girls were not treated as important in that culture. So Mum said to me, 'Look, you and your brother probably need to go back to live on the border. Live near Poipet because then you can probably find a way to get across the border to Thailand, because if we all stay here together, we're going to die.' "

The Pol Pot regime hand-picked from their own people those families who could go back to the border area in order to grow rice and wheat for the soldiers and authorities. They also made sure that those selected to live near the border were those who would not wish to escape across the border. Therefore, they picked their own people who were Cambodian, and not those whose background was Chinese or another minority, so Te's family was not picked. But his mother knew a family that was Cambodian and qualified to go and live on the border, so she bribed them. Te doesn't know how much money she paid, but they took Chheng and Te to the border in September of 1975.

"We didn't know this family, but in order to become part of their family, we just had to keep lying to the authorities. This was difficult because we looked different. We had much whiter skin and the real Cambodian has a much darker skin. However, that family had received money from my mother, so they had to keep their promise to her.

The Khmer Rouge stopped the whole family and pointing to me said, 'What is this Chinese kid doing in your family?' The Cambodian parents lied to the authorities by saying that 'Their parents are dead already. We just picked them from the street and they have become our family.' The Khmer Rouge believed this story and so we were allowed to pass and we travelled not quite to the border, but back to the town Donorang that we first lived in as refugees."

In Donorang, crops were still growing, so they had corn, bananas and other fruits to eat for the rest of the season. Te and Chheng now belonged to the 'government' along with everyone else, and they were soon separated from their host family and from each other. Chheng was placed into a young peoples' camp and Te was placed with a group of teenagers. They got to see each other at night though because the camps used the same kitchen area. It was a massive kitchen serving about one hundred families. They each had one plate and one spoon and would line up for food. During the day, they worked in the rice paddies under the guard of the Khmer Rouge. They dug the ground and planted the rice in straight rows. They worked hard.

Chapter 5
Death All Around – 1975-77

Chheng and Te managed to stay together up to two years by seeing each other at night in the camp. That was up until 1977 when Te was eighteen years of age and he was taken away because he was no longer regarded as a teenager.

"My brother was still young at twelve years of age and I didn't know if he would understand what I was saying to him, but this was the last of our family now separating. It was heartbreaking to be losing my only remaining family member.

I remember that we were talking at one of the temples in Cambodia which was in the town Donorang. Right by it was this big massive tree – we call it Bo-Tree[8] in Cambodia. So I

---

[8] Sometimes called the Sacred Fig; this tree is a species of banyan fig native to India, Bangladesh, Nepal, Pakistan, Sri Lanka, southwest China and Indochina. It is a large, dry season-deciduous or semi-evergreen tree up

said to him that 'No matter what happens, if we separate, one day I will find you and come and look for you by this big tree.' He said, 'Okay,' and that was it. That was the last time I saw him."

The Khmer Rouge took Te about forty to sixty kilometres away from the camp and his brother. They placed him in a group of bigger and stronger workers aged 18 to 30. There were about 300 or 400 people in the group, and they were required to do farm work. They were treated more harshly and worked harder because they were more grown up. They were considered the 'top' workers. They lived in make-shift houses, huts or tents so they could be mobile. They never stayed in one place for more than a month or two. They built their own huts or slept in hammocks tied between two trees. They worked like slaves sixteen hours a day.

"If you died on the job working and you didn't make it, they didn't care. I saw lots of people who died. Some died because there was always sickness amongst us, or they were overworked and didn't have enough to eat because food was very limited. I saw people being killed and tortured. You feel fear. Constantly. They would kill people in front of you as a way of teaching you to behave and stop doing certain things such as a man and a woman having a relationship or liking each other. They would even shoot their own people. They would take people away quietly in the middle of the night and

---

to 30 m tall and with a trunk diameter of up to 3 m. The leaves are cordate in shape with a distinctive extended tip; they are 10–17 cm long and 8–12 cm broad, with a 6–10 cm petiole. The fruit is a small fig 1-1.5 cm in diameter, green ripening to purple. The Bodhi tree and the Sri Maha Bodhi propagated from it are famous specimens of Sacred Fig.

kill them because there was some suspicion that they might have been educated or a government official, for example.

I remember one day there were guns going off. I don't know who was fighting or what was happening, but I remember bullets falling around us like a shower and people all dying around me. We all ran, but people were dying next to me. I looked at the sky and wished for Grandma; Grandma gave me strength. One day I see all these teenagers around me and the next day, they are all dead. How did I survive all that?

You didn't have a life. Instead, you went through each day hungry and you lived in fear. You never had any idea of what might happen the next day. It is hard to describe my life at that time. You just thought about surviving and you dreamt about going back one day to your home and being happy again.

Of course you couldn't complain. Whatever they were giving you, you just ate what was available. Anything that you see, you eat it. You see an insect and you eat it. Definitely, there was no stealing. If you were found stealing, they would just shoot you on sight. Everyone was affected. Sometimes, I never thought that I would get out of this. I just thought that we would die and be left or buried. 'When are we going to die?' I would ask myself.

If they also thought that the people didn't somehow respect them in what they were telling them to do, then they would just shoot those people, too. They would just shoot you on the spot. They said to us, 'That's what you're going to get if you don't listen to what we say.' Every time they think people are not listening to them or don't want to do what they were telling them to do, then they would just kill those people. Then they would say, 'See, that's what happens if people don't listen to us.'

I saw many people killed like that in front of me. I can't count how many, but I saw many such killings. I saw more than ten of these murders every month right in front of me and not just one person each time. Sometimes I saw them kill a whole family. I saw this a number of times. I did not want to see these things. However, they told us we must see the killings. We all have fears and traumas of all of this that we still have with us today. We all have the fear still, inside of us. The fear of what we have seen and experienced.

Everybody had this fear. We never trusted other people because you didn't know who you could talk to. Sometimes in a group there could be one or two spies. The spy would be one of us, and they become a spy because they thought they would be treated better. We didn't know, though, which person was a spy. So not trusting other people was always there, but we just lived to survive.

I would see my friends die. I saw six couples shot in front of me. There were to be no relationships between a man and a woman and you were not allowed to 'like' a woman. Men and women were separated to work in different fields. However, at night we would come back to our huts – one long hut for the men and one for the women, both made out of bamboo and palm leaves. They would watch you to see if you had a connection with someone. I remember when they called all of our groups together – about three hundred people or more – and we were told to sit down and watch. They called some people to come and stand out in front. Then the general would stand on a tree stump above the crowd and announce, 'We warned you from day one that there was to be no secret love between a man and a woman.'

They did not want you to be in love. So they said to us all in the big group, that this is what happens to you if you break the rules and have a connection. The Khmer Rouge would each have an AK rifle and they would fire one bullet through the head of each of the couples. I saw a bullet go through each person's head. I peed in my pants but didn't realize it until afterwards. Everyone was so scared. Women would collapse seeing these killings. You carry these images with you for life. You see it time after time and you become used to it. The first time, though, was with these couples. I'll never forget it.

Some of the workers would say things like, 'What's the point? We're all going to die anyway.' We were all so skinny and we were constantly tortured. We were also constantly supervised and watched. If you pretended you were sick, you were warned once. The next time, you would just disappear and not be seen again.

There were other problems I faced, too. People singled you out if you looked different. I looked different because I had whiter skin. Before the war started, a lot of people had said that because I had a different skin colour, that I probably came from a better family with a privileged background. At the time, I wasn't sure if my skin colour worked against me. I wasn't sure of the meaning of it all, but I sensed that it started to work against me. They started to be suspicious of me that maybe I came from a more privileged and better background. I thought originally that they were probably only killing the people who were lazy or didn't listen to what they were told to do. Beyond that, I didn't know much about why they killed some people and not others.

I had an idea that they might be targeting certain people. It didn't occur to me that they were purging out particular races or classes or cleaning out particular races or cultures. Originally, when Pol Pot started to cleanse all these different classes of people I was only in high school. When they approached me, though, in the killing fields, I did not understand what they were trying to do beyond killing the people that they said were lazy. I knew that I was part of a wealthy family, but I didn't tell them. One of the supervisors would call a person over and interview them. One of those supervisors would see certain things that would make them want to interview a specific person.

Grandma knew that the Communists would come into Cambodia. Every night she would tell me about the Communists coming in through China. Grandma had told me many things, but I always remember Grandma saying, 'Look, you children need to listen to what I say, and that's fine. If you don't listen to what I say, that's okay. But I'll just say it anyway. If they do come to Cambodia, just remember what I told you. The Communists are always the same.'

Then ten years went on and when the war came I realised how Grandma had really known that Cambodia was going to be in that sort of situation and that was what she had been telling me. So I think that without her telling me all of those stories I wouldn't have survived. That's how I was really able to get past the tests that the Khmer Rouge put me through day in and day out. I thought of Grandma at the time telling me, 'If they ask you this or ask you that, you just don't tell them. You just don't tell them the truth. If you tell them the truth, you'll be dead. Try to act as dumb as possible.' So, I got to be good at acting and pretending how poor I was and that I was from a working family.

We never knew the reason why one person was interviewed. It would seem to come from nowhere. The supervisor approached me and asked, 'Are your family wealthy?' And I told him no. He said, 'Are you going to school?' I told him, 'I go to school but just normal primary school – I've never been to high school.' He asked me, 'Can you read the newspapers and books and things like that?' And I said, 'No, I cannot read.'

So when they handed me a book or a magazine or something to read, I said, 'No, I can't read.' They said, 'But you look like Chinese. You have got a white skin. Your skin is so white.' I could read, but I lied to them. This was to save myself because I knew that something was going on. I lied all the time to protect myself. I said, 'Well, my skin being white doesn't mean my family is a very rich family. We come from a poor family.' That's the thing they didn't like – if they knew you were either rich or educated or that you were somebody that was really well known – that's when they would kill you.

I said, 'I come from a country town. I come from Kokolot.' I told them, 'Okay, I look white. It doesn't mean that I am a rich kid.' I told the supervisor that I was from Kokolot, but I didn't tell him that my family was the Tang family. If I had told him he might have known my history, so I told him my name was Te. He made many attempts to ask me, interview me, and ask me who my father and my mother were, where they were, and I just said to him that they'd been killed during the war, during all of the bombing and things. So when they heard that my mother and father had been killed and that my other family members had been killed as well, they felt a bit sorry for me because I was pretty much still a child.

By now I thought that something was really going on. It was just like Grandma used to tell us when the Communists ruled in China. She would tell us about the Communists. They hated the rich, so they cleansed the land of the rich. So I came to the conclusion that the Khmer Rouge would be just like Grandma was telling us about how the Communists were. It was fortunate that I remembered what my Grandma said. But the rumours had already started at that time because of all the killings and all the injuries that were happening. We all knew something was different – something that we didn't expect would ever happen. We'd seen killing, but it was more than just that. It was a cleansing. I was able to survive at the time because I didn't have my brother with me or my parents with me. So when they interviewed me, they didn't know who my parents were because we were all separated as a family.

For me to describe this to people who don't really know much about the war in Cambodia is very hard. I never imagined how we could live life like that either. You live through it, you go through that sort of torture with the starvation and hard working and really it's just unbelievable. So it's the small details I really can't describe. I try to forget it. It was so hard."

Chapter 6
Survival – 1977-79

They worked sixteen hours every day at a lot of different tasks, but mostly they dug in the rice paddies. If they wanted to smoke, they grew their own tobacco from seed, and were allowed ten to fifteen minutes rest to smoke. Otherwise they had to work all the time.

They were given two digging poles of different widths – like picks – to carry and use all the time. If they lost a digger they would be in big trouble. They were also given a cotton towel to use as a sarong, a tea towel, and as a towel itself. They each had two pairs of black pants and two black shirts which were usually replaced every three months or so.

"We slept wherever we were at the time and sometimes that meant we slept in the water. We had to build a dam to stop all the water flowing through from Thailand. All this water had to be dammed in order to make paddies. They tried to make paddies maybe three times a year instead of one time a year.

But then the dam broke. We had to work in it and fix the dam. I felt so tired. We all felt so tired. And we just had to sleep in the water. So we just dig those two poles into the mud and we sleep in the middle so you don't get swept away with the water. We sleep tied to our poles with our towel tying us in. You never knew when the flood water would come, and when it did, it would come quickly. We couldn't go to the high ground or hills to sleep because of the snakes, pigs and other animals. Poisonous snakes can't swim so we were safer sleeping in the water.

There were trees as well. But we can't sleep in a tree because of snakes up there. Everything was done in the water in the paddies. You work there; you sleep there. You do anything to survive at the time.

It is just like…we all were like asleep really. We were so hungry that we didn't think so much about death now, we thought about what we could do to eat and survive – every day the same. We'd get up. We'd go. We worked. We would just say we don't know when it's going to be our turn, you know, to be floating around dead in the water.

We saw people dying. You see all this water flowing past you and then you see all these bodies every day. We never knew when it was our time. We don't know from which town the bodies were. You can see people floating past you and we were talking that we don't know when it was going to happen to us. We always say we'd never survive. None of us, you know."

One day in 1979, the workers in the fields heard a big bang, like a bomb, quite a distance away. They didn't have radios of course, and they never heard any news about anything from other towns or the outside world, but it sounded like there was fighting going on. At night they saw lights flashing all over the sky. Over the course of the next week the fighting got closer and closer and the noise louder and louder. Based on what they had been told in past years, they guessed that Americans were waging war on their country.

"We can't live like this any more and we say whatever that is, whatever the noise is, we want to see what's going to happen. One morning we were still working as normal, and we could hear these bombs, but the Khmer Rouge tried to tell us nothing was happening, that it's just part of training. But we do not think it is normal."

Then they saw a long line of tanks and heard a shell coming straight toward them. With that, they all ran for the big river nearby. The river was lined with mango trees, their jumbled roots reaching into the river itself. They jumped into the river and climbed up into the roots, shells landing in the river all around them, the blasts so loud they could hear nothing else. They tied themselves to the mango roots, and there they stayed all day and all night. They could hear the Khmer Rouge running past, frantic commotion and people yelling, 'They're coming, they're coming!'

"We did not know at that time who was coming. The Pol Pot were running away, but we don't know who 'they' were. 'They' were not the Pol Pot.

But we were all in black – all black uniforms – both civilians like us as well as the Khmer Rouge soldiers. The whole country was all black and I assumed the tanks would not know who we were. How could they tell the difference? They were just shelling all of us."

Then the Khmer Rouge were gone and the teenagers and workers were left behind, hiding along the river bank.

Chapter 7
Vietnamese Army Liberates

TE and the others came out from the mango trees and the river bank with their hands up to find that they were surrounded by Vietnamese soldiers. One of the boys spoke Vietnamese, so he raised his white towel and shouted, "All these people are civilians. They are not soldiers." A soldier said, "As long as you don't have guns, it's OK. Just go on and stay away from the fighting."

One soldier however, walked toward Te and asked him, "You're not soldier?" He said no.

"Okay, have you got any brothers or sisters?" Te said yes.

"How about your mother and father?" Te said, "They are all gone. Separated."

"Are any of your family here?" Te said, "No, only myself."

"Okay, so where are your family then? They are all gone? They are all die?" This soldier knew about the Khmer Rouge because the Vietnamese army had come this way before. He asked, "Do you know if your parents die or not?"

Te said, "I don't know. We all got separated one by one. I've got my brother, though. My brother was in the next town to me the last time I saw him two years ago."

He said, "Two years ago?" Te then told him how his family's separations occurred and how he had survived the four torturous years of the Khmer Rouge occupation. The soldier became very emotional and started to cry.

Then the soldier said to Te, "Okay, from now on you don't go anywhere. I'm going to find your brother for you. Tomorrow you're going to stay with this tank." He pointed at a huge tank. This tank was much bigger than all the others. "I will take you to find your brother." He told all the other soldiers, "Tomorrow you take this boy and I don't want him dead. I want him to see his brother."

After the conversation, another soldier from one of the tanks came and shouted across at Te, "What did you tell him? Why is he crying?" Te said, "I just tell him my story. You know, how my family separated and so on." He said to Te, "Do you know who that was? That's our general." That soldier had never seen his general cry. That's how Te found out that he was actually talking to the general.

The next day, the fighting started again. The tanks shelled ahead of themselves and moved on. They took about six or seven hours to move forty or fifty kilometres, Te walking behind the tank.

"I saw so many things. I saw corpses, body parts and blood everywhere. The tanks just run over the bodies. The Khmer Rouge are just lying there and the tanks run over them. It's just like we're all animals. But I don't really think so much about it at the time because the only thing I wanted then was to see my brother. I was always thinking whether I'm going to find him or not and that's what keeps me going and it's always inside of me. I say to myself, 'No matter what, I still remember. No matter what, I will find you by the big tree.'

Then when the tanks get to the town, I see all these bodies lying around. You name it: dog, cat, human. Bodies – I don't know how many thousand – because the tanks were shelling days and nights; shelling ahead of us before we could get there. It was smoky and hazy and things were burning. There was death all around."

They reached the town Donorang at about five o'clock in the afternoon. The general said to Te, "I hope he's not dead, I hope your brother is here."

"I don't know what to say to him. I went to the tree and then we saw that the temple next to the tree was gone. It is destroyed; flat to the ground. But there's the Bo-Tree still left there. I don't want to look for a body in case it was my brother Chheng. I was there about a couple of hours waiting for him to come. Obviously everything had then quietened down. It was getting dark.

About half-an-hour later I'm looking into the smoke and haze. There are some lights in the distance and I saw someone walk past that smoke, from maybe a hundred metres, maybe one hundred and fifty or two hundred metres. We were sitting on top of the tank at the time so I could see pretty much clear, and the land was quite flat, and I say, 'That looks like my brother.' Maybe I was just thinking about it and said it, but then I looked again and I saw him walk towards me, because he was coming to the tree, you see. So he kept walking towards me and I say, 'That is definitely my brother.' The closer he comes I'm sure that's him. I thought he might be skinny, but obviously he's okay, because he's had more food than I had. Maybe it's because he's a bit smaller or younger and they feed him better. So anyway the general asks me, 'Are you sure that's him?' I said. 'Yes, that's him!' I couldn't believe it. They all applaud for me!

So, I got down off the tank. I just go over to him and I say, 'Do you remember that I tell you? Go to the tree and I find you?' He said that he remembered. He said he came two days ago before we got there. It's 1979 when I meet him again and we were separated in 1977.[9] Back then he was about ten or eleven years old when we were separated. I was about nineteen or twenty years when I found him. I can't imagine how I found him when I'd lost everyone else – it's a miracle that I found him when I'd lost everyone else. So that's how I found my brother again.

So there's just two of us together at last, my brother and I. I don't know where any of my family are except my brother Chheng who was with me and who I met at the big tree. My young brother and me are together again!

---

[9] Today Chheng is 45 years old and lives in Adelaide running The Bangkok Restaurant.

A photo of Chheng and his wife Ao when they were married in Bangkok in 1998, standing behind Te and Sanom both seated with Kevin in front.

Chapter 8
Our First Thailand Refugee
Camp – Finding Part of My Family

Every day after that Te thought that somehow he might find the rest of his family. He now had some hope. Finding his brother was a miracle for him. So, he and his brother planned to go into Thailand to a refugee camp. With six or seven other teenagers, they made their way through Northwest Cambodia to Sisophon in West Cambodia. One night they came across Vietnamese soldiers guarding a big petrol tank at Nimith and they decided to stay there. There were other families and children already hiding there in bunkers as well. They dug themselves a bunker to sleep in for the night and for extra protection dug it near the petrol tank itself since it was being well-guarded.

But the Khmer Rouge were still fighting the Vietnamese in guerrilla pockets, and through the night the fighting started again and bullets flew all around. If the petrol tank had been hit, it would have exploded and they would probably have all been killed. Not one bullet hit the tank, but the Vietnamese however, got pushed back and left everyone else hiding in the bunkers. The Khmer Rouge knew the bunkers were occupied and progressively threw grenades straight into the bunkers. They murdered all the families and children in those bunkers. There was a full moon and Te was very worried they would see his shiny black hair and blow up their bunker, too. But his group huddled together and were missed by the Khmer Rouge.

"I smelt the blood, the gunpowder, and the burnt flesh, and bodies of those murdered. The Khmer Rouge are the killing machines. In the morning when we climb out of the bunker, I see body parts up in the trees and scattered all around us. How we survived I do not know. Someone is watching over us. God is watching over us, this I believe.

When I think and talk about it now I can still smell the blood and the burnt bodies. It comes back to me instantly. Five years ago, I travelled with Sanom to show her the towns around the Angkor Wat where I was during the killing fields. As we flew into that area, I looked out the plane across the rice fields and the jungle and I was fine. But once the plane landed and I smelt the land, it all flooded back to me and I burst into tears.

One day it is my dream to save up my money and go back to this area around Sisophon in Northwest Cambodia, and to travel back there with Sanom. In particular, I really want to visit Donorang where I met my little brother Chheng under the big tree, and walk that track back to Nimith again. I know that I will be very emotional, but it will be a special moment for me. I want to experience those emotions again and ask again,

'How is it that I survived?' You need to believe in miracles; they happen sometimes."

They wandered for about a week, making their way to Sisophon. They ate anything that was available, because they knew they had to survive that walk. Cambodia does have a lot of produce, and there were always fruit trees. And they were able to scavenge chickens and beef that had been left behind. The land no longer belonged to the Khmer Rouge, and they didn't have to steal any more.

Thousands of people tried to flee Cambodia and cross the border. They didn't know what to expect under the new rule, because the Vietnamese had been the enemy of the country for an extended time. The Vietnamese and the Cambodians had a very poor history and everyone felt unsure about the future. They never imagined a day when it would be the Vietnamese who would actually free them.

When they finally got to Sisophon, they found the family who originally looked after Te and Chheng in the town of Donorang where the Bo-Tree was. Because they had lost their loved ones, this family offered to adopt them and be step-parents to them. It is Cambodian custom to adopt children because they help "protect" the family's natural children. This family had only one remaining son. They were very kind to Te and Chheng and looked after them well. Because the family was originally from Siem Reap in Angkor Wat, they all made their way there.

"Food is very scarce and a few of us teenagers went out to look for food. We walked along the jungle tracks into the Angkor Wat temple area. This is an area of spirits because it is so old and ancient and you need to talk and behave respectfully in this area. We walk and walk, but cannot find any food. We finally walk up to and through the large entrance gates of the temple and then we walk down into its centre. At the very centre is a large Buddha statue, but with the bombing and the war the head has fallen off onto the ground. The six or seven of us boys lift it back onto the statue itself and then we make a wish for food.

As we walk back on the same track that we came in, we suddenly see lots of taro trees which are food for us.[10] How is it that the food is there now? Is it because of our wish? We are so happy to find food, so we dig up the roots for the taro. But as we do, the Khmer Rouge who are still in the area, see us and start to shoot at us and then we just run. The hail of bullets is so strong that it cuts down all the taro trees next to us as we run. The taro trees all fall over as we run. We run back to the Angkor Wat gates where the Vietnamese tanks are standing guard and they see us running, but they do not fire because they see that we have no guns. They wait for us to run past them and then they take aim and fire at the Khmer Rouge. We are safe, but still no food.

It is amazing that I am still alive. I must have been dead at least ten times. But as I said, someone is watching over me."

One day in Siem Reap, Chheng ran up to Te saying, "Come, come, come!" He said that he had seen their half-brother, Tang, on the road. Te went quickly and discovered Tang and his half-mother and half-sisters, Bi, Bouy, and

---

[10] Taro is a root vegetable like a form of potato.

Chang.[11] Bouy was married before the war started so she also had four children with her, as did Chang; eight nephews and nieces altogether!

"Now that I had found my half-mother, both Chheng and I left the other adopted family. The mother of that family was very sad to see us go. She told me that I was a special kid and that she had never seen anyone so busy and so good at making money and being able to survive.

Now that we were with my half-mother, we needed to have a plan about what to do. We could not go back to where Grandma had her land, her house, her farms and her rice factory because once the war had ended in that area, people just took over the land. One of my family had said that they had gone back to that area where Grandma lived, but it had all been taken. So we stayed on in Siem Reap and lived there for seven months."

The Khmer Rouge were still fighting in the countryside and jungle, but the main roads were now safe. The family however, made a decision to try to go into business again. Te's half-mother gave him her gold ring; the only thing that she had left. The plan was that Te would walk back to the Thai border about 160km to Aranyaprathet in Thailand. He knew that area well from before the war when he had done business there as a teenager. With that, he made his way to Sisophon, about 45kms from the border sticking to the main roads. In order to get to the actual border though, he had to travel with the

---

[11] Bi is currently living in Melbourne in Victoria, Bouy is in Parafield Gardens in South Australia, and Chang, who lived in the USA, died in July 2009 from a heart attack.

Vietnamese patrols for safety. One evening, he joined about a hundred others on their way to the border, sleeping with them under the Vietnamese general's house. (The houses in that region are all built on stilts.) As it happened, the general needed someone to be an interpreter for him, and he was very pleased that Te was able to do so.

He told Te that if he would help him with interpreting during the trip to the border, he would waive the escort fee that all the others had to pay. Since Te had only his half-mother's ring, which eventually sold in Thailand for about AU$10, this was a great stroke of fortune. Again, someone was watching over him.

So, Te finally got to the Thai border, about 160km, to Aranyaprathet in Thailand across from Poipet.

When Te crossed the border into Thailand, he pretended he was Thai, bought some sarongs, put them in his bag and walked back to Siem Reap to sell them there. He had to make many trips to make any substantial income, and that's what he did numbers of times for the next four months.

He made enough money though, to buy a bicycle so he could make more trips and faster. He imported cigarettes and watches, not only because they were light to carry back, but because those items were in great demand in Cambodia after the war. He became quite prosperous.

Te & Bouy pictured together in 1995.

Te Pictured with his half-mother Tang Huy Chuy in the late 1990s.

After about seven months in Siem Reap, the family decided to move to Sisophon, back closer to the Thai border. They wanted to get into Thailand, but they had to be very careful; though the Vietnamese protected Sisophon itself, the Khmer Rouge were still fighting in pockets south of there. There was still fighting on the highway from Sisophon to Poipet. To get to the Thai border therefore, they would have to go north through the jungle for about forty or fifty kilometres and cross a rather large river.

Te knew the way, and so they decided to break into two groups to ensure that the family would endure if something happened to one of the groups. First he took his half-mother and Chheng, plus six of the younger nieces and nephews. Their parents, Bouy, her husband Kong, Chang, and her husband Monghong stayed behind. At the river, Te had to take one child at a time across. All the nieces and nephews still remember to this day what Te did for them on this perilous journey. However, there is another adventure that they will never forget either.

"On this trip, there was no water in the jungle and it was too dangerous to go out into the open spaces to get water, so their mother turned to me and said, 'You let the children drink your wee.' I said, 'Are you kidding? You really sure?' 'Yes,' she said. To this day, my nieces and nephews still remember drinking their uncle's urine."

When both groups made it to the Thailand border, they took refuge under plastic sheets, branches and anything they could for about a week until representatives from the United Nations found them and took them to a temporary camp at Aranyaprathet.

After another week, Chang's family were actually selected to be refugees to go to another country, though no-one knew where they would be going at that stage. This all happened very quickly. A bus was therefore sent to pick up Te and all his family to transport them to Bangkok. Chang's family were the first on the bus, but the bus filled up and the rest of the family missed out going on that particular bus. They were told that another bus would be sent the next day to pick up the rest of them.

Three of those nephews and nieces are shown here in Las Vegas in 2009; the first on the left and the third and fourth from the left.

The next day when the bus finally arrived, it started out for Bangkok following the same route as the previous bus with Chang's family on it, but halfway there it was stopped by soldiers who directed the bus instead, to a refugee camp called Sakaeo 1. They were all supposed to be going to Bangkok, but the soldiers weren't informed of that.

How life can change in an instant. One decision by some soldiers changed the course of Te's life.

Instead of heading for a new country, for the next two and a half years, Te and his family lived in refugee camps in Thailand.

Te's group learnt much later that Chang's family had been taken to Bangkok and then direct to the United States of America to be settled there. "If I had been on that bus, I would now be living in the USA!"

"And if I had gone straight to Bangkok on that bus, and if the soldiers hadn't redirected us, I would never have come to Australia and never have found my natural sister Suree."

Chapter 9
Our Second Thailand Refugee Camp – Finding My Natural Sisters

I t was now 1980. The group stayed in Sakaeo 1 for about four or five months. Both Khmer Rouge refugees and "Freedom Cambodian" refugees like Te were all in this camp together.

After a few months however, and once people got back to better health and regained energy again, conflict arose between the two groups.

So the Cambodians were moved to the Mairut refugee camp, closer to the coast.

A group of refugees in Mairut Camp; Te is in the white shirt, standing right behind the bicycle.

Te worked with the United Nations as an interpreter because he spoke Chinese, Cambodian and Thai. And it was at Mairut that he learnt to cook. There were five or six women in the kitchen who cooked for the Thai navy officials, the ground troops' generals, and the UN officials. The kitchen was purpose-built for the high-ranking officials. Te became friends with these women while he was there. At one stage, they asked him, "Te, you want to learn cooking?" And Te answered yes. That's essentially how he got started. They taught him how to cook over about eighteen months from about 1980-81. Te says that those skills in cooking are still with him today in his restaurant.

"As an interpreter though, I was helping with people who were sick and needing care and interpreting for them. You name it and I was helping in the situation to interpret. One time after we had been there for about three months, I was walking inside the camp on one of the roads and I saw somebody walk past me, but then they looked right past me. I was walking one way and they were walking the other way, but then I thought to myself, 'Gee, this looks like my sister.' I'm talking about a girl that's got no hair left on her head − not one hair − at that time she was bald, because she had gone through all this malaria and diarrhoea and you name it − and she is also so skinny and has a big tummy. She walked past me, but it was the face that caught me − the face was still there − and then I knew. She looked like my sister, you know, and she walked right past me.

But she is thinking the same as me − because I've put on a bit of weight already after being in the camp for about three months. She was thinking the same way that I'm thinking. He looks like my brother you know, she says to herself. So she turned around and I turned around and I said, and she said to me 'You, you!'

That was unbelievable, for me. Yes, marvelous! For me to meet my sister again in one particular camp and for the United Nations to take her to my camp from amongst 20-30 other camps is unbelievable. Later, there were hundreds of refugee camps all along the border. But I end up in that camp where she is! So that's how I first met my second sister. My natural sister, Suree.[12]

But I then said to her, 'What in God's name has happened? What in God's name?' She had gone through all this starvation, fleeing through all the jungle with the Khmer Rouge. She didn't escape like us at the time. When the Khmer Rouge ran all the way to the jungle away from the Vietnamese, she followed them.

She didn't pick the signs.

So she didn't know **not** to follow them. A lot of the workers followed the fleeing Khmer Rouge, just going along with them and they all ran through the jungle and that's what she did. They all fled to the Thai border, but just on the Cambodia side. She said she thought she was dead.

---

[12] "Her real name is Ching. Her name is Ching with one 'H'. My brother is Chheng, there's two 'H' in his name. So Ching, that's her real name. She changed her name though. I don't know when exactly, but it was when she got to Australia that she called herself Suree. She's the one that opened the Suree's Thai Kitchen in Hyde Park, Adelaide."

Standing with two others in the refugee camp with Te on the left and Suree on the far right; this was taken much later after their first reunion.

So that's how I find my natural sister Suree (Ching). It was about a couple of months later that we heard the news of some more of my family – my other natural sister, my eldest sister Lang! I was working for the United Nations and I knew this lady called Barbara. Barbara worked for the Red Cross and she also worked for one of the United Nations agencies called UNHCR [United Nations High Commissioner for Refugees, which protected and supported refugees and helped resettle them into other countries]. Barbara knew a bit of my story so she saw a name in this other Thai camp – that's where my eldest sister was found. As soon as she saw that name pop up – Te – Barbara knew that it was my sister. So she came to my camp – she flew back to our camp in a helicopter just to tell me, 'Te, I've found your sister, your eldest sister!'

Lang[13] was married during the Pol Pot time. I didn't know that when I first met her again in the refugee camp. The last time I had seen her she was single. She also had two children during the war period. She hadn't wanted to marry when we were all separated as a family, but she decided to anyway."

The UN had helped Te's family members come together at Mairut, and now there were seven of them together again: Te, Suree, Lang, Chheng, Bi, Bouy, and Tang. They were there for about two years with about 70,000 other refugees.

---

[13] Lang is now in Adelaide and owns and runs the Phuket Thai Restaurant at Glenelg.

Chheng, Suree and Te (on the right) in the refugee camp.

Refugees were flown out to countries like Canada, the USA, Switzerland, France and Australia. Lang was the first one in Te's family to come to Australia. She arrived in Adelaide in 1981. Her mother-in-law had arrived before her, in late 1979 or early 1980, at the beginning of the Vietnamese invasion – probably one of the first refugees to make it to Australia. Then Lang became a sponsor for Te and the rest of his family.

They had to go through a screening process for settlement in a new country. They passed the interviews and were moved to a third camp called Churburry at Parnutnekum. They passed all of the health checks there and after six months were approved to move to Australia.

Once cleared medically, they were sent to a fourth camp called Saun Plu, which was in Bangkok on the same street as the Australian Embassy. They waited there about a month, during which time Te continued to work for the UN two or three days a week.

They were now all full of hope about going to Australia.

Taken in Las Vegas in 2009, Te is on the left; back row on the left is his half-brother Tang; second row in the middle is his eldest half-sister Bouy; front row on the left is his eldest natural sister Lang; in front second from the right is his half-sister Bi.

Chapter 10
Touchdown in Australia

Te tastes freedom and can scarcely believe it. "I arrived in Melbourne on Qantas Airlines on February 6th, 1982. I still remember that it was hot that day, forty-two degrees. When we landed and the door to the plane opened, I wanted to go out because I could see the freedom. From the time the door opened, I just said to myself, 'We are free. We are free.' Even though it was so hot, I could still feel the freedom. I had never had that feeling before, that feeling of freedom. I can't explain my emotions at that moment. I'll never forget when we first arrived in Australia.

When we went out of the airport and out through the main door, the heat all hit us and we all went, 'Oh!' and rushed back inside the airport!"

Te, Chheng and Suree had been sponsored by Lang and had arrived together. The next day they took a bus to Adelaide. Te remembers that the heat wave was also going full blast in Adelaide. They were on the TV news and in the newspaper called *The News*. Te still has the clipping from the paper in which they told about how they survived.

They were hosted first at the Glen Osmond Passionist Monastery for about six months, during which Te did a bit of schooling and learned English. Father Christopher Mithen was at the Monastery then, and really looked after Te's family. Father Chris was there for about ten years before moving to Tasmania and is now located in Melbourne. He still travels sometimes to Adelaide to visit. His fifty-year anniversary as a priest was in 2008, and Te visited with him at the monastery in Adelaide to celebrate.

As well as Father Chris, the other person who really looked after Te in those early days was a person called Tony Keenan who worked as a Welfare Officer under the auspices of the Monastery Refugee Project at Glen Osmond. As Te recalls, Tony apparently helped to re-settle and reunite families as well as assisted people to look for both housing and work.

In 1983, Tony asked a group including Te if they would like to earn some money during the school holidays. Te was 23 at the time. Te agreed and asked what they would do for the work. Tony said they could do some fruit picking, and though they said that they had never done that kind of work before, Tony said they could "give it a try."

They would not have to work all the time, just during the school holidays. So they went to Barmera and Loveday in the Riverland area of South Australia to pick fruit. Barmera is on the main highway and Loveday is a little town outside Barmera.

"The News" 16/2/82 p.14.

Refugee family together again

A Kampuchean woman who thought she had lost her two brothers and sisters in Thailand has been reunited with them in Adelaide.

By Linda Cook

Mrs Te Quech Lang of Adelaide had given up hope of ever seeing her sister, Te Bouy Chheng, and brothers, Te Thao and Te Cheng, again after 1975.

The family was split with the occupation of Phnom Penh by the Khmer Rouge, and sent to do forced labor on farm collectives.

In 1979, during fighting between the Khmer Rouge and Vietnamese-backed Heng Samrin forces, Mrs Te, pregnant with her second child, Taing Seay Ty, her husband, Taing Veng Kong, and Taing Huy Hieng, 2, escaped over the Thai border.

The Taings found shelter at the Red Cross refugee camp at Yalan, but after a month, were driven back to Kampuchea by Thai troops.

Flight

They returned to their home-town, Baottambang, a 1500 kilometre walk which took them about three months, but were unable to trace Mrs Te's parents and relatives who had also left for Thailand.

After a second successful flight from Kampuchea in 1981, the Taings were taken to Khao I Dang and later Mairu refugee camps.

It was at the second, three days after their

Mrs Te Quech Lang (second from right) reunited with her sister, Te Bouy Chheng, and brothers, Te Thao and Te Cheng

arrival, that the astonished Taings discovered Mrs Te's brothers and sister were also in the camp.

"It was such unbelievable luck, it gave me a feeling of somehow being in the hands of Providence," Mrs Te said today

"We had four very happy months together, although we were sad nothing had been heard of our parents, before my husband and I were found a new home in Australia last April.

Tony took them there and Te still remembers that his boss' name was Alex. Tony asked the boss, Alex, "Do you have any jobs for these people?" At first Alex said, "Oh, no, no, no; we don't want any Vietnamese here." Tony said, "These people are not Vietnamese. They are Cambodian." Alex replied, "What's the difference? They all look the same." Tony said, "They're different. They are not Vietnamese."

Tony said, "These are refugee people. They are from Cambodia. They just want to experience what it's like in Australia. If you take them on, I can guarantee you that they will work hard for you, and if you think they're going to cause you any trouble, you can call me any time and I will come and pick them up. Here's my business card." So Alex finally agreed and took the four of them.

"Alex gave us a caravan and we lived in it. On that first morning, he took us to the vines. We'd never seen a vineyard before. I had seen grapes for sale in the market, but I had never seen a vineyard because Cambodia didn't have them. Alex said, 'You have obviously never picked grapes before then?' I told him that it was my first time to see a vineyard and he replied, 'Okay, if you can finish this row here I will pay you $150.' At the time, in 1983, it was a lot of money.

I had a picking partner named Saroo and he was also from Cambodia. We worked together, him on one side of the vine and me on the other. So we figured that if we finished that row we would have $75 each, not bad for a day's work. At the time, we didn't know how long the row was and didn't have any idea where it went because it went up and over a ridge. We started picking at 6am and picked pretty much all day until 4pm. We worked until we got to the top of the hill and thought that the row would end at the top of the rise. But when we got to the rise we saw that the row still went on. We said, 'Oh, sugar, after that we've still got another way to go.' So we kept picking until 9pm and the sun went down.

That next morning, we got started at 5.30am, right as the sun was rising. The sun wasn't out yet, but you could still see the grapes. That day, we picked two rows. I still remember that Alex said, 'How is that possible? Your first day you finished at nine and only did one row and now, how can you finish two rows in one day?' He said that nobody could do that and he and his wife walked from one end to the other, checking all of the vines to make sure we didn't leave anything behind – they were very expensive grapes!

I didn't know it at the time, but Alex actually called Tony. Tony told me this later and said that he thought Alex was calling him to ask him to come and pick us up. Tony asked if we were giving Alex a hard time and he said, 'Oh, no! Have you got any more Cambodian kids there?' Tony laughed and said that he had five more and asked if he wanted them." Those five worked at Alex's father-in-law, John's, farm. Te remembers John as a really nice man, welcoming and understanding. Tony decided to have a holiday as well, so he worked there too on John's farm for a bit of an adventure with the "Cambodian kids."

One of those "kids" now owns a restaurant called the Thai Orchid in Adelaide. Another one is in Sydney and owns a grocery store. They all have their own businesses now.

Tony made six dollars an hour before taxes, while Te was working under contract. The more Te picked, the more he made, and he worked hard enough that he actually made more money than Tony.

"There is a funny story to tell about our time at the vineyards. When Tony was picking at John's farm he said, 'We hardly have a day off,' and John said, 'Look, you guys can't work every day. You've got to take one day off – Sunday is a family day, your friends' day. You all go out together and have some Aussie pub beers and play some games or something. Go and watch a movie.'

So one Sunday afternoon we all went to a pub with Tony. There were about ten of us. When we walked in the door, it was pretty much a full-on pub with the Aussies watching Sunday footie and drinking beer, and all of a sudden they all went quiet. You could hear a pin drop. Tony said, 'Look don't turn back, just walk straight through to the bar and order your drinks.' We all walked straight to the bar and they all leaned toward us. The barman came down and said, 'Okay, guys, what would you like to drink?' And we said, 'Can we have a Coke?' That was the first order. The second one ordered Coke, the third one Coke, and then the bartender said, 'Don't tell me you are going to have ten Cokes.' We all said yes, and then we drank our Cokes and left. We got out of there.

So that next Sunday, we did the same thing. Tony asked if we wanted to go back again and we said yes. This time, the bartender said, 'Oh, are you guys going to have ten Cokes again today?' And we said, 'No, no, no; we're going to have beer today.' It was so hot out there. So from that Sunday on we went to the Barmera Hotel and drank beer with all of the Aussie locals. They were all farm owners and fruit growers as well and we introduced ourselves. There was John, Bob, Tony

– there were about ten Tonys in the pub and twenty Johns in the pub and Bobs, you know. I asked Tony, 'Gee, how many Johns are there in Australia?' Tony replied, 'You know, it's just like your name here – how many Tes, how many Tangs, how many Wongs are there in Asia? – it's just the same. Here it is normal.' But, yes, every Sunday we would go and have a beer and we played snooker, and that's how I learned about footie. Tony was a Crows supporter.

Working at the vineyard really gave me confidence. Alex said to me, 'Te, I've been on this farm for thirty-odd years, and I've never seen anybody work as hard as you do. For me to see people work like that is just incredible.' It felt good to hear my boss say that and it gave me some credit for what I had done for him in one season."

Te's journey including his work and his adventures in the Riverland were recently reported in *Insight Magazine* in "The Sunday Mail" (see the article on the next page).

Te didn't go back after that season of grape-picking, instead he began his life in earnest back in Adelaide enjoying his new country. However, he certainly didn't feel like his first taste of work in Australia was a hard life at all. He had freedom and he was happy.

THE RESTAURATEURS: Te Thao (left) and Bunna Ngov at one of their favourite spots, Henley Beach jetty. **Picture:** Patrick Gorbunovs

Article from *Insight Magazine*, "The Sunday Mail," 19th June, 2011, page 46.

TE THAO
BUNNA NGOV
CAMBODIA

BUNNA and Te are two mates with much in common: born in Cambodia, grew up there and survived the hell that was Pol Pot's notorious Killing Fields where an estimated two million people died at the hands of the Khmer Rouge and through disease and starvation.

When working in the rice paddies, Bunna, now 50, was only 14. "The horrible thing was that if you were alive, you didn't know when you were going to die," he reflects.

"You just wait for your turn next, to die. You never think you'll get out ... that is the nightmare every night you sleep.

"They can kill you tomorrow, not just starve you to death. They can kill you any time they wanted. Maybe they don't like you, or you don't perform well because you don't have the energy to do really hard work, then the next day, you get killed. And that was day by day."

Bunna lost a brother and sister on these fields.

Te, 51, lost his parents in the same way, but was reunited with a sister in a refugee camp where he was working as an interpreter.

"All the refugees were lining up, I walked along the line and I walked past someone and I think, 'that looks like my sister'," he says.

"But she had not one hair on her head and a bloated tummy. She was nearly dead. I turned around and said, 'is that really you?'.

"That face, I could never forget. For almost five years we had been separated because she was elder than me. I couldn't believe it. I thought she was dead. To have your sister in one camp, is like a million chance to one."

After meeting in a refugee camp in Thailand in the late 1970s and the early '80s, Bunna and Te have made lives for themselves in South Australia, forging even greater friendships as Thai restaurateurs: Bunna owns Henley Beach's Thai Orchid and Te the Regent Thai, in North Adelaide. And their common traits have continued in their adopted home: they are both big Crows supporters and they don't mind a game of poker, either. Bunna and Te have learnt with hard work – including fruit picking in the Riverland – anyone can be successful.

"It wasn't hard to start life in Adelaide," Te says. "The war in Cambodia, that was hard."

Te says when he first arrived, some growers in the Riverland were sceptical about hiring Cambodians. They were given a one-week try.

"First day, we went to the vineyards. I had never even seen wine before. Cambodians don't have wine. We were told we would get $150 per row we picked. But we didn't check how long the rows were," Te says.

"Another friend and I started picking about 5am, and we picked until 4pm and we got to the top of the hill and we saw the row kept going over the hill and down in the distance. We thought, 'oh no'.

"It was hard work, but still it was a new start and that kept us going. It was nothing compared to what we'd been through.

"We finished the row at 9pm. Some people who had worked picking these same vines, it took them three days to finish. We did it in one day, and the next day we picked two rows. We just worked like you would not believe it.

"So he called in and asked for more Cambodians to come work there."

It goes to show, that hard work really does pay off.

Chapter 11
The Start of the Restaurants

A fter the work in the vineyards, the group went back to Adelaide and Te worked at the Genghis Khan Mongolian Restaurant on Glen Osmond Road. This was in 1983. At first he was a dishwasher, and then about six months later he became a chef.

"I cooked in the big wok with the long chopsticks. It was a lot of fun. It was really my first taste of a full-time job. I worked there for about two years, right up until 1985.

Fortunately, my future brother-in-law, Peter Thanissom, who married my sister Suree, approached me one day in 1985 and said, 'Te, would you be interested in a restaurant?' I said that I couldn't afford one and Peter said, 'Look, I'm going to move my restaurant down to Rundle Street. Are you interested in Regent Arcade? You can have my position there. Just pay me a bit every year – whatever you can pay me.' He said that compared to what I was making, it wouldn't be a lot of money, but he wanted me to start a business."

Chheng Te (left), Suree Te, Thao Te and Quech
Lang Te . . . sticking together

Desperate quest for refugees

THESE brothers and sisters, reunited after being separated in refugee camps, are still searching desperately for their parents.

"But we are so lucky to be together," sister Quech Lang Te said.

They searched faces for four long years, hoping to find each other or their parents after being separated in various Cambodian border camps.

Although they found each other, they could find no details of their parents' whereabouts.

They don't know if they are living or dead.

"We don't even have photographs of our parents – everything was burnt," youngest brother, Chheng Te said.

"But it would have been dangerous to have any identification, because we are Chinese."

It is now 15 years since they were separated from their parents, Taing Huy Ant and Te Nam Chang.

Refugee Week has triggered fresh hopes that someone has heard of or seen their parents.

Their tragic separation and survival struggle has drawn them together.

"We've had some very hard times. But things will get better," said older brother Thao Te.

The foursome opened a Chinese restaurant in Glenelg last year.

The New Thursday June 28/6/90. 11

Te called his restaurant the Angkor Wat after the temple in Siem Reap in Northwestern Cambodia, the gateway to the world famous heritage site of the Angkor temples. He wanted his restaurant to be part Cambodian and part Thai because he had lived on the border. Both Thailand and Cambodia have similar foods and culture. He ran the Angkor Wat from 1985 until 1990, and during that time, he married his first wife and had two daughters.

In 1990, the Regent Arcade decided to renovate and didn't want restaurants there any more. At the same time, he was going through a tough period and his marriage also ended at that stage. His family had encouraged Te to marry, but the two weren't really in love. When he left, he gave her the restaurant and everything else out of concern for his children. She moved the Angkor Wat to Grote Street and thought that she could run it, but it went broke after a year.

"My first marriage was very difficult. Those years that I was married to her were a sad part of my life. My current wife Sanom and my family have supported me in continuing to support my daughters, but it has been a hole in my life. I loved and supported my family from the very beginning. But it's difficult when you've got someone breaking your heart and you're giving them everything. They got the house, the car, everything. After a while, they still did not appreciate what I was doing for them. That's when my own family said to me, 'How stupid can you be?' In the end, my former wife wound up bankrupt anyway, but it was still hard to see my children suffer.

I don't see my daughters very much. For me, back then I didn't want to fight anymore. I went through one war and it taught me a lot. I didn't want to fight. I said to my ex-wife, 'I don't know much about this country at all, but whatever is done, is done. For me though, I just want to see my children. Just let me see my children.' She was smarter than me and had more education and probably knew more about the law than I did. That's what she thought anyway. I said that I didn't want to fight anymore. I didn't have the resources to do that. I had nothing left. I gave her everything because I just wanted to see the children, but in the end, I didn't get to see them. And that's why it's left a hole in me.

Linda is now twenty-five and I haven't seen her for about five years now, and Jessie is twenty-three, and I haven't seen her in three years. They used to live in Adelaide, but they left about eight years ago. Linda lives in Canberra because she works there. Jessie probably lives in Melbourne now with her mother. Their grandparents all live in Canberra. Jessie calls me sometimes, but we don't have a close relationship. Her mother took that away from me. I tried, but I didn't want to go through with all of the lawsuits. I paid their child support until they were eighteen, but for their mother to take them from me, she really had no right to do that. But the door is always open to them at any time. They are still my daughters and I love them.

For me, if those two children would ever come and see me, I will tell them, 'If you've got any problems you come here. You've got a home here. If you want to work with me, that's ok with me. As you know already, I've always been a restaurateur. That's all I can do. But you can do your education here if you want, you can do school here. I will support you in whatever way I can support you.' So I would give that guarantee to them. I'm not forgetting them. Hopefully one day..."

Once Te left the Angkor Wat, he went to help his sister, Lang, with her restaurant in Glenelg called the Phuket Thai Restaurant. Sanom was a waitress there, and they had met when she worked occasionally at the Angkor Wat. Te's brother was married to one of her friends. She had been a student in Adelaide and helped Te get through some difficult times after his divorce. She seemed to make sense when they would talk together and she always gave him good advice. They eventually married in 1992, and were the first Cambodians to be married in the chapel at the Glen Osmond Monastery. Father Chris arranged everything – the church, the flowers – everything.

"I started from scratch again. I started saving money and had the support from my family. I found a business called Adelaide Thai – before that it was called The White Crane – located right on the present spot at O'Connell Street, and I offered them money for it, but they wanted too much. Later, they came back to me in February or March of 2000 and asked me if I was still interested in the price that I had offered and I said yes."

Te changed the name to the Regent Thai, thinking customers that knew him from the restaurant in Regent Arcade might make the connection with this present restaurant. "When Sanom and I took over the restaurant in early 2000, we worked down at the Phuket at Glenelg during the day and then for a couple of months we came to North Adelaide at night to clean this restaurant until two or three in the morning. On 27th July, 2000, we opened the Regent Thai right in North Adelaide at 165 O'Connell Street. We have just celebrated our first ten years at North Adelaide! What a ten years!"

for you DOUG REINEK'S

DINING

Sunday Extra

Delicious survival for brave family

Just your average, everyday, horror story — but with a delicious ending.

When Pol Pot's murderers came to town the Te family was forcibly broken up.

They became slave labor during the madness of Cambodia's ghastly Year Zero.

Against the odds, probably in the order of a million to one, the four children, Lang, Suree, Thao and Chhang, survived.

Against the odds once more and quite by chance, they were reunited in one of the refugee camps on the Thai border.

To this day they do not know what happened to their parents.

But they have a new home in Australia and they have opened the Phuket restaurant at Glenelg.

Adelaide is well endowed with quality Thai restaurants, the venerable and glorious Bangkok, Star of Siam and the recently opened Sala Thai being my favorites.

ABOVE: *Chhang Suree, Lang and Thao Te ... opened Glenelg's Phuket restaurant*

Phuket is of like, which is to say first class, quality.

It is on two levels, small downstairs and spacious above, with a separate take away operation.

The food is Cambodian-influenced Thai, lots of spice and for those who like it hot, lots of chilli fire.

With that old faithful Jim Barry riesling, we started with a couple of stars, a strong powerfully flavored prawn patties with a cucumber salad and ground peanut and larp gai — finely minced chicken with bags of herbs and chilli.

The menu lists fully 50 dishes from tom yum soup to coconut ice cream.

Our main plates were some scrumptious egg noo-

dles stir fried with bean sprouts, spring onions, egg, chicken and soy sauce which could have been a nourishing light lunch in themselves.

Then a dish which was new to us, moo gratium prig Thai or pepper pork, the meat braised with garlic and ground pepper and given the touch of sweetness which goes so well with pork. Despite the name, the flavors were mild and lovely.

Full frontal fire (they checked whether we liked bags of chilli) came with a beef curry on the menu as neau phad prig khing. The beef was curried with stir fried bamboo shoot, chilli and vegetables. Served with lots of gravy to soak into the rice, it was our kind of nosh.

Given all that they been through and their sheer guts I would be disposed to recommend the Phuket to you anyway.

But hand on heart I assert that the recommendation is based very firmly on the quality of the food and service. Nice people, nice new Australians.

☐ WHERE: Phuket, 162 Jetty Rd, Glenelg. Phone 295 1903.
☐ WHEN: Lunch Tuesday to Friday; dinner nightly.
☐ WHAT: Jim Barry riesling (2) $29.60; larp, $4.60; prawn patties, $8.40; rice, $1; noodles, $8.50; curry, $9.80; pepper pork, $8.60. Total $68.70.

Healthy ways to eat all you fancy

AUSTRALIA'S best known fish fancier Peter Doyle — of Doyle's restaurants on Sydney Harbor — makes a contribution to public health with a new book A Little Of What You Fancy (Milner $12.95).

It started when he found he had a high cholesterol reading. Something had to happen.

The result is a book written in breezy

fashion and including some very useful recipes. Not all are fish-centred by any means; they range from cheese dip to apple and mango jelly and they include some using liquor.

Perhaps the best recommendation I can offer is that Peter Doyle has lost 30kg since his change of lifestyle.

Another is that the book is endorsed by the National Heart Foundation.

guide to GOOD LIVING

Te celebrates life! – Te and Sanom at Te's 50th birthday party in 2009.

The Regent Thai as it looks today.

"It was hard in those early days, but I do owe a lot of gratitude to my accountant Frank Cutillo, who was with me in those very early days and he has stuck by me. He helped me market the restaurant and was always giving good advice about what to do.

The restaurant was slow in those first months. I remember for example that it was the first of October, 2000, and the only people in the restaurant that night were Frank and myself sitting at a table by the window. But the customers started to come and Frank, too, got all his Italian friends and family to come. Sometimes there were so many Italians in the restaurant that I wondered if I was running a Thai or Italian restaurant!

Frank in the white shirt and tie at Te's 50th birthday party with partner Elana on the left and friends Bronwyn and Rob Dundon on the right.

One of the things, though, that did really help to bring customers was that Tony Baker, the food and wine writer, came to our restaurant for lunch one day in August of 2000, and really loved it. He published an article in *The Advertiser* called "Welcome Joy" and that helped turn things around. By the end of that year, we never looked back.

Now we have lots of regular customers and the restaurant is busy most nights and full on weekends. If the restaurant is a little slow, the take-away is busy. So it is going well and we did not feel that we lost any customers during the global financial crisis. They all stuck by us and we stuck by them!"

eating out / regent thai

Welcome joy

THE time: the late-70. The place: a refugee camp inside Thailand on the Cambodian border. Two men pass each other. There is one of those not quite-sure moments and, so physically changed by deprivation are they, it takes a minute or so for the emaciated brothers to recognise each other.

A few months later. The place: another refugee camp inside Thailand on the Cambodian border. The first man walks past a slight, also emaciated young woman. She sees who he is. Only after her cry of recognition does her brother turn around and realise she, too, has survived. Their parents are dead, for these are the human remnants of Pol Pot's killing fields. Totally against the odds, separated and

enduring years of hideous deprivation, the four surviving siblings of the Te family made it. The oldest sister found a welcome in Australia – Adelaide. The others were reunited as part of a program which makes me proud to be Australian.

But these are the pages of the suburban restaurant to the food. Those lucky but, above all, plucky survivors today run four separate and fine Thai restaurants. Suree Te became Suree Thanitsorn, and Suree's Kitchen in Hyde Park is superb. Her elder sister Lang Te's Phuket at Glenelg is grand. Cheng

Te took over the Bangkok Restaurant in the city started by South Australia's king of Siamese eating, Peter Thanitsorn, and thrives.

Regent Pai mixed entree

And then there is Savorn – supply. I hope this is not a too elaborate preamble to introduce that first refugee. That Te, who with his wife Savorn has just opened Adelaide's newest Thai restaurant. I think you should go there now. Go there now or ... with a happy ending but because you deserve as good a meal as we had.

The joy of Thai food for us is that the flavours are fierce (not necessarily after) fresh, positive, at once

FRESH Thao Te and wife Savorn.
Picture: GRANT NOWELL

separate and harmonious. At risk of seeming a pariah, it is akin to swimming a time yet being able to distinguish each spice.

The room at Regent Thai is on the face of it, just another of the O'Connell St strip, commodious, comfortable, with its peach shades and pleasantly dressed tables and undreatening Thai cutlery. Welcoming and with edible joy on the plates and in the bowls.

I must acknowledge that Mr Te knew us and was aware of our errand and so perhaps he had gone to a spot of trouble to ensure the freshness of his chilli crab.

Reader, ring ahead. Make a booking. Insist on such chilli crab if crabs are offering themselves for sacrifice on our shores. After all these years of ecstatic, perfect take may glance upon this marriage, I had not realised the extent to which Lili Baker is a glutton, a shell-sucking, time-probing glutton. Very bad news for crabs.

Shortly before, Thao Te produced a plate of scallops in shells with the subtlest of soy-based sauces enhanced by a vegetable julienne. We, then drank from the Shell. One of the cliché dishes of the diaspora of Thai restaurants is mussaman curry, derived from the southern Islamic communities of that largely Buddhist world: merchant's nirvana. Regent Thai's mussaman chicken

as those crabs did of Lili. As for the Thai noodles, at the table at our last supper – the meal we order when the last exit beckons – one of the terminal forkfuls will be impaled on such noodles. It is worth adding for a substantial minority of the readership that they also have a separate vegetarian menu. With similar, perhaps greater, enthusiasm, I add that the wine list includes a more than decent house bottle at $12. If only other places would follow suit.

Pol Pot was vile, evil. He caused the Te family, and so many other families, horrors we can only imagine. The hideous man did, however, deliver us a favor. The Te haven is grand news for foodies.

TOM RIVER

The Menu

Starters
Prawn tostas $8.50
Pandan chicken $7.50
Seafood soup $6.50
Amber rolls $6.50

Mains
Red beef curry $14.50 (?)
Ginger chicken $12.50
Peppercorn seafood $14.50
Stir noodles $11.50
Gong sang $13.50
Chilli fish $17.50
Steamed rice $1.50

WHERE: Regent Thai, 145 O'Connell St
North Adelaide, phone 8267 6627. O...

WHEN: ... day, Mon-Fri, dinner nightly

IN A NUTSHELL: Terrific Thai

RATING LILI: Food 9, serving 9, value 9.

Te and Billie Reed at a Restaurant Awards Night in 2008.

In 2005 and 2006, Regent Thai was a finalist in the Restaurant and Catering awards in South Australia. In 2007, it won the award for the best Thai restaurant in Adelaide. That was a very proud moment for Te and Sanom.

"We had worked so very hard with no holidays. But we feel very honoured to serve our customers. Many of them are regulars who always support us and they also bring their friends and family which makes us very proud, too. We are honoured to serve them and give them good food."

Photo of the Award from 2007.

In April of 2008, they renovated their restaurant because it had the same décor as when they first opened in 2000. While talking to Billie Reed one night, (Billie is in real estate now in her own company, but she is an interior decorator too), Te mentioned that he and Sanom had not had a holiday for three years. They wanted to go to Thailand, and he asked if Billie would decorate and paint the restaurant if they closed it for two weeks while they went to Thailand. Billie agreed right away and Te brought out a bottle of champagne to celebrate. The next morning Billie met with them at her office to discuss what she could do. The following week he and Sanom left on a plane to Thailand.

Photos of the interior of the renovated restaurant.

"When I came back I could not believe it. It had all changed in two weeks. I cried when I saw it. I was so happy. I was so proud of my new restaurant. My staff were so proud, too. It is so good to work in such a lovely place with good customers. I am so thankful.

In 2009, I turned fifty years and I decided to have a party in my restaurant. I first went to dinner in another restaurant where I didn't have to worry about any of the cooking, but I took my own spicy sauce – the more spicy the better – and I had it on a nice large steak. Then we came back to the Regent Thai for desserts and the restaurant had all been decorated with balloons. It was good to celebrate. I never thought that I would live when I was in the killing fields and I never thought that I would get to fifty and I never thought that I would be able to live in freedom like we can in this country. It was good to celebrate."

Te enjoys his 'spicy' steak with friend Vin Pearce.

Julie & Alf Brown at the 50th Birthday Party.

Photos from Te's 50th Birthday Party at Regent Thai.

Chapter 12
Finding My Father

Mr. Tang who currently lives in Adelaide, was a long-time friend of Te's father. In 1997, Mr Tang went to Saigon, Vietnam, to see his own family. Incredibly, he recognised Te's father there in a market place, even though he hadn't seen him in thirty years. They talked about the good old days in Cambodia and because Mr Tang now lives in Parafield Gardens in the northern suburbs of Adelaide, he, of course, knew Te's family.

Te's father had gone back to Cambodia to look for his family, and was told that they had been killed. Mr Tang assured him that they were, in fact, alive and in Australia now and told him about the restaurants and businesses they owned. Te's father was in disbelief. He found it hard to believe. Afterall, he had been told his family had all died and had believed this for almost 20 years.

Mr Tang came back and told Te and his family how he had found their father. They didn't believe him at first either, but Mr Tang showed them a picture of him.

Te's father came to Australia on December 26th in 1997. He had another lady by then, and three more children – two boys and a girl – who still live in Vietnam because they cannot get entry into Australia at this time.

"Dad told us that he wasn't in Cambodia at the time when the Khmer Rouge invaded. He was in Saigon doing business at that stage and he couldn't get back to my mother. He told us his story. Otherwise, we wouldn't know.

He said that two weeks before the Khmer Rouge took over our country, he came to see us in Poipet. He then went back to Phnom Penh, then went to Vietnam on business, but once the invasion happened, he couldn't get back into Cambodia. The borders were closed. For four years or more, he had to stay and live in Saigon while the war continued in Cambodia because the border was shut. When the Vietnamese invaded in 1979, Dad came back to Cambodia to look for his wives and children, but was told that they had all been killed.

Sadly, my father passed away in Adelaide on the twenty-ninth of April, 2011. Dad was ninety years of age. A few months before, he had stopped eating. It was almost like he was saying that he'd had enough. It was time for him to go.

We still have not found my mother, but after twenty years or more we did find my father, so who knows? Maybe one day. We are still looking. Mum would be maybe in her seventies if she was still alive. But there is hope. Always hope."

Te with his father and son Kevin in 1997.

Chapter 13
My Family in Australia

Family is important to Te. "Once you have been through what we have been through, you know how important family really is. Family really matters.

Of course, I have my wife Sanom and my son Kevin. Kevin is now nineteen years and completed Year 12 at Blackfriars College in 2009. We are very proud of him. He started to do a diploma in hospitality at Regency Technical and Further Education, but is now doing accountancy instead."

Te with Sanom and Kevin in 1994.

Te's family consists of the following.

His natural siblings who are with him in Adelaide are:

Lang, his eldest sister, who owns the Phuket Thai Restaurant at 162 Jetty Road in Glenelg, the seaside suburb in Adelaide, South Australia;

Suree, his next eldest sister, who owns Suree's Thai Kitchen at 330 Unley Road in Hyde Park, a suburb of Adelaide;

and **Chheng**, his younger brother, who owns the Bangkok Thai Restaurant at 199 Waymouth Street in the CBD of Adelaide.

It sounds like they have all the Thai restaurants in Adelaide! Te's half-siblings from his father's other wife are:

Bouy, his eldest half-sister, who owns the Hong Kong Hardware store north of the city of Adelaide at Parafield Gardens;

Chang, his elder half-sister, who lived in Los Angeles in the USA. Chang died of a heart attack in September of 2009;

Bi, his elder half-sister, who runs a take-away restaurant in Melbourne;

Tang, his younger half-brother, who worked at ROH, a wheel and rim factory in Adelaide for twenty years. Due to the economic downturn in 2008 he is unemployed, but is re-training in computers;

and **Hunh Chang**, his half-brother, who was killed by the Khmer Rouge along with his grandmother in 1973.

Te's **half-mother** lived with Te and Sanom in Adelaide for about twenty years, but died in a car accident in China in the late 1990s when she was there visiting relatives.

His **father** recently died in 2011. He has five nieces and nephews in the USA and he has five cousins and relatives now living in France and five more living in Switzerland.

"You cannot replace family. You understand how important family really is once you have gone through the horror of the kind of war that we went through.

I just cannot imagine how my family can be united in this way because I have seen so many other thousands of families never make it. How is it that I had so much luck in comparison to so many other families who have lost everyone and everything? I'm just very lucky in comparison to so many other families. I'm so thankful.

And to me – to me it's just unbelievable. It's beyond my wildest dreams. How can it be that I get all my brothers and sisters back through that war-torn country, through soldiers killing millions? So that's why sometimes I think that I don't know what to thank or whom to thank – somehow, some way, someone is really looking after our family so well. I just say to myself, 'It must be God or somebody who looks after our family.' Sometimes I just pray to Grandma and Grandpa – whoever – just to look after us up there. I just thank them.

Yes, from time to time when I was in the killing fields, I would have to run through bullets being fired and I just say to God – and to Grandma – 'Help me.' And the bullets just passed me by – the bullets just went past me – so I know it's just not human. I see bodies lying around me sometimes; those bodies are of someone that I met maybe half-an-hour before and we are talking and all of a sudden he's dead and I'm not.

It is all that sort of thing. That's what makes me grateful. When the war was on, all I really wanted was to get to find my family. Sometimes I was also thinking how lucky I am compared to thousands of other families that never made it. I still have a lot of friends who never found their parents or never found their brothers and sisters up to this day.

We are all grateful that we made it here to Australia and that Australia is a great country. There is opportunity here. There is freedom and opportunity that we could never have imagined that we could ever have had when we were in the war in Cambodia.

I am so grateful that I am here in Australia with all of my family. I am so grateful to be a survivor and I am so thankful to all those people, including family, friends and customers, who have supported me over nearly thirty years in this country.

To all of you, thank you. Thank you."

Te, Sanom and Kevin in 2010.

The restaurant website can be found at www.regentthai.com.au

Made in the USA
Coppell, TX
28 September 2024

37820389R00069